Animal Icons

GRAY WOLVES

Sheila Griffin Llanas

ABDO Publishing Company

CHECKERBOARD ANIMAL LIBRARY

ANIMAL ICONS

visit us at
www.abdopublishing.com

Published by ABDO Publishing Company, PO Box 398166, Minneapolis, MN 55439.
Copyright © 2013 by Abdo Consulting Group, Inc. International copyrights reserved in all
countries. No part of this book may be reproduced in any form without written permission
from the publisher. The Checkerboard Library™ is a trademark and logo of ABDO Publishing
Company.

Printed in the United States of America, North Mankato, Minnesota.
112012
012013

 PRINTED ON RECYCLED PAPER

Cover Photo: Shannon Bauman
Interior Photos: Alamy pp. 1, 6–7, 8, 10, 22–23, 26–27; Getty Images pp. 16–17; Glow Images
    pp. 12–13, 14–15, 18–19, 20–21, 28–29; iStockphoto p. 9; Thinkstock pp. 4–5, 10–11, 24–25

Editors: Rochelle Baltzer, Megan M. Gunderson, Stephanie Hedlund
Art Direction: Neil Klinepier

Cataloging-in-Publication Data

Llanas, Sheila Griffin, 1958-
 Gray wolves / Sheila Griffin Llanas.
  p. cm. -- (Animal icons)
Includes bibliographical references and index.
ISBN 978-1-61783-571-1
1. Wolves--Juvenile literature. 2. Gray wolves--Juvenile literature. I. Title.
599.74--dc22

                2012946817

CONTENTS

GRAY WOLVES

One night in 2008, a biologist howled into the sky. He and his team waited. Back across the Cascade Mountains came a low, deep reply. A wolf!

The excited biologists recorded their data. Their discovery was important. It meant wolves had returned to Washington State for the first time in 70 years.

The team did not see any wolves that night. But the howls were proof enough. The gray wolf's trademark is its howl. Wolves howl to call family members and warn off strangers. That night the wolves seemed to say, "Yes, we are here!"

The gray wolf's range once extended from Alaska to Mexico. In the United States, gray wolves lived from coast to coast. But hunters tried to get rid of them. As wolf populations disappeared, conservationists learned a big lesson. Nature needs these top predators.

Today, gray wolves live in the Rocky Mountains and near the Great Lakes. They also live in Alaska and Canada. The gray wolf is a symbol of the wilderness. It is an animal icon.

A gray wolf's howl can travel as far as six miles (10 km).

An icon is a cultural symbol. Animal icons stand for the people and land of nations, states, and cities. Animal icons are shown on flags and signs. They appear in songs, legends, and stories. They represent history. They teach people about nature and about themselves.

GRAY WOLF HISTORY

Gray wolves have been around for thousands of years. They are found in North America, Europe, and Asia. Long ago in Europe, gray wolves prowled the forests and frightened villagers. Stories of werewolves spread. And, people told fairy tales. Wolves were seen as evil in stories such as "Little Red Riding Hood" and "The Three Little Pigs."

European **immigrants** brought stories of the "big

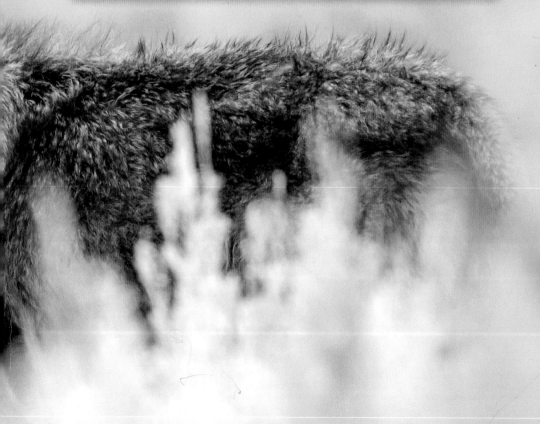

The gray wolf is also called the timber wolf.

bad wolf" to North America. There, settlers disliked wolves because they sometimes preyed on livestock. Wolves did this more as humans hunted their foods, including deer and buffaloes. In turn, people hunted, trapped, and poisoned wolves. Many people wanted them gone altogether.

Scientists believe that thousands of years ago, people bred gray wolves to be less aggressive. The pet dogs we know today descend from these wolves.

7

By some estimates, 250,000 wolves lived in the United States when settlers arrived. By 1900, wolves were mostly gone from New England. And by the 1930s, they had disappeared from the West.

Between 350 and 700 gray wolves survived in northern Minnesota in the 1960s. A few more lived in northern Michigan. They were the last wild wolves in the **continental** United States.

People who supported killing wolves felt they had done the nation a service. However, people eventually realized wolves play an important role in their ecosystem.

Slowly, conservationists and writers began to change people's views of wolves. In Jack London's *White Fang*, a wolf

More than 65,000 wolves live in North America today. The largest populations are in Canada, Alaska, and Minnesota.

Where gray wolves live

becomes a loyal pet. Wolves save a girl lost in the tundra in *Julie of the Wolves* by Jean Craighead George.

In 1967, gray wolves were listed as **endangered**. But today, wolf populations are growing. In 2011, Oregon counted 29 wolves. Washington is home to eight wolf packs. Minnesota claims more than 3,000 wolves, while about 1,500 live in the northern Rocky Mountains. In Alaska, there may be as many as 11,000.

MORE LORE

Stories about wolves are found wherever wolves live. In one ancient tale, twin boys Romulus and Remus are left to die. They are saved by a wolf, who feeds them. They go on to found the city of Rome, Italy, at the place where the wolf discovered them.

A Quileute wolf headdress. Author Stephenie Meyer wrote of this tribe and its stories in her Twilight novel series.

Wolves also play a large role in Native American mythology. The Kwakiutl creation myth tells of men and women taking off their wolf masks to become people. Wolves also appear in Quinault and Makah creation myths.

In a Ute legend, a wolf carries people in a bag on his back. When he sets down the heavy bag, it breaks open and people run out to live on Earth. In the Quileute creation myth, the first tribe members are changed from wolves into people.

Native Americans respected gray wolves as guides, brothers, and hunters. Wolf packs represented the value of family bonds. Wolves are such expert hunters that some tribes even used wolf skins when hunting. These important animals also appeared as artwork on everything from weapons to rock walls.

TAIL TO HOWL

Gray wolves look like large dogs. Like dogs, they are members of the family **Canidae**. Their scientific name is *Canis lupus*.

Male wolves are larger than females. Males stand about 30 inches (75 cm) tall at the shoulders. They are up to 6.6 feet (2 m) long. The tail is 1.5 feet (0.5 m) of that length. Males range from 70 to 145 pounds (30 to 65 kg). Females weigh 60 to 100 pounds (25 to 45 kg).

Gray wolves have short ears and large, blocky snouts. Their piercing eyes are gray, green, or gold. Wolves have very keen senses of smell. They also have good hearing and vision.

A double layer of thick fur keeps wolves warm. Their coats range from white to black. The fur is lighter on the belly and face. The long, bushy tail often has a black tip.

These big animals are built for travel. Wolves can trot for long stretches at five miles per hour (8 km/h). They run for short sprints at up to 40 miles per hour (64 km/h). Their paws leave tracks that are four by three inches (10 by 8 cm) across.

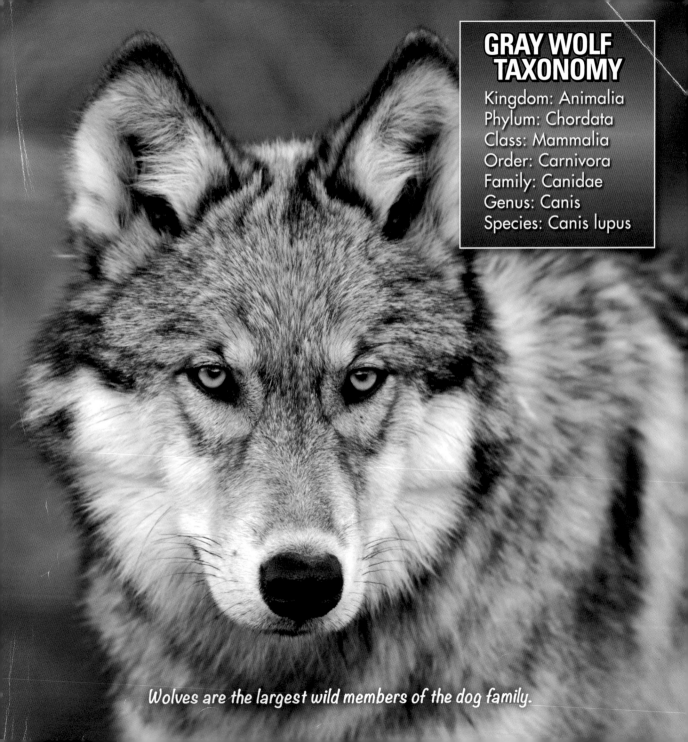

GRAY WOLF TAXONOMY

Kingdom: Animalia
Phylum: Chordata
Class: Mammalia
Order: Carnivora
Family: Canidae
Genus: Canis
Species: Canis lupus

Wolves are the largest wild members of the dog family.

WHAT'S FOR DINNER?

The gray wolf relies on its ability to travel to find its prey. These carnivores travel up to 30 miles (50 km) a day in search of food. They may be on the move for up to eight hours a day.

Gray wolves prefer to eat 5 to 14 pounds (2 to 6 kg) of meat a day. They can go hungry for more than two weeks. But when they find meat, they gorge. Each wolf might fill its large stomach with up to 20 pounds (9 kg) of food at one time!

How can wolves find such a large amount of meat in one place? Their main food source is ungulates (UHNG-gyuh-luhts). These are large hoofed mammals such as deer, elk, moose, and buffaloes.

Gray wolves also eat bighorn sheep, caribou, beavers, and hares. Some Canadian wolves even eat salmon! Wolves may eat smaller prey, such as mice, but this is rare. Gray wolves are known to kill livestock such as cattle, sheep, and turkeys. This habit makes them unpopular with some ranchers and farmers.

Wolves can smell deer up to one mile (1.6 km) away.

Gray wolves hunt mostly at night. They chase far more animals than they catch. The hunt may take several hours for large prey. But once the prey is caught, they kill it in just a few minutes.

Wolves have 42 teeth, which is 10 more than humans have. Each of their four fangs are up to 2 inches (5 cm)

Gray wolves drink lots of water.

Wolves are good swimmers. They will follow prey into water, even in winter.

long. These bite through skin and grip prey. Sharp side teeth cut flesh. Wolves use their flat back teeth to grind and mash food. Wolves bite down hard! Their jaws can break a buffalo's leg bone or a moose's skull.

Wolves eat a lot, but their hunting helps keep large **game** herds healthy. They take old, sick, and weak members. For wolves, these animals are the easiest to catch. In this way, wolves help herds of other species stay fast, strong, and healthy.

Wolves also help feed other animals. Other species **scavenge** their leftovers. Coyotes, bald eagles, and grizzly bears all eat what wolves leave behind.

GRAY WOLF
BEHAVIOR

Wolves live with family members in groups called packs. A male and female, the alpha pair, lead the pack. Their offspring and other adults make up the rest of the pack.

Wolves are social animals. They show each other affection and become very attached to one another. They use body language and sounds to communicate.

To call a pack together or keep strangers away, they howl. When two or more wolves howl together, they never stay on the same note. This creates a larger sound. Scientists think wolves do this to make the pack seem bigger.

Often, communication relates to the social order that exists in a wolf pack. When two wolves meet, the dominant wolf stands tall with its tail aloft. Its ears are up and forward, and it growls and bares its teeth. The **subordinate** wolf crouches with its tail between its legs. Its ears turn down and it may whine. It may also roll on its back.

Wolves are very smart. As keen observers, they watch and learn from one another. When one wolf learns something, the rest of the pack learns it too.

Wolf communication helps strengthen the social order of the pack.

Most gray wolf packs have 8 members. But, pack size can range from 2 to 30. A big pack needs a lot of food. If there is not enough, pack members may leave. A wolf may join another pack or start its own in a new territory.

Pack size is connected to territory size. And territory size depends on how much food is available. Territory size can also change depending on the season. A pack may claim 30 to 1,200 square miles (80 to 3,000 sq km) of land.

Wolves mark their territories with urine and feces. The smell tells other wolves to stay away. If strangers trespass, they may be attacked. Sometimes, wolf packs agree to share a border. However, territories rarely overlap by more than a mile.

Wolves thrive in tundra and woodlands. They live well in forests and grasslands. They survive in swamps, mountains, deserts, and barren lands. They can live anywhere they have enough food.

Living as a pack is the reason gray wolves can take down large prey.

BIRTH TO DEATH

Wolves usually mate for life. The alpha male and female **breed** in early spring, between February and April. A mother wolf is **pregnant** for 63 days. She gives birth to a **litter** of five to six pups in a cozy den.

Newborn pups are helpless. They cannot see or hear. They weigh just one pound (0.5 kg). But as their mother nurses them, they grow. Pups live in the den for about two months. Then, they spend their time in the open at areas called rendezvous sites.

Soon, the pups are ready for real food. After a hunt, adult wolves swallow meat and hurry back to the pups. There, they **regurgitate** the food for them. By fall, pups are ready to hunt with the pack.

After two to three years, some gray wolves leave the pack. If prey is plentiful, they choose a new territory close

All pack members care for pups.

to their birthplace. If prey is scarce, they may travel as far as 600 miles (965 km) seeking a new home.

Gray wolves can live up to 13 years in the wild, but most do not. Pups are at risk of illness and starvation. Adults also face conflicts with other wolves and injuries from hunting.

Wolves may dig dens. Or, they may use caves, hollow logs, or abandoned beaver lodges.

23

THE ICONIC GRAY WOLF

Over time, wolves have shown themselves to be survivors. These intelligent creatures sit at the top of the food chain. And, they have survived efforts to get rid of them. Because of these admirable traits, wolves are a powerful symbol.

In Ontario, Canada, a roadside attraction features two wolves and two moose. The sculpture reminds visitors of the ongoing cycle of predator and prey.

The modern Pawnee Nation flag and seal also bear the image of a wolf. It represents **cunning** and courage to this Native American tribe.

The courage of wolves inspires a few football teams, too. The University of New Mexico athletic teams are the Lobos, the Spanish word for wolves. North Carolina State University athletic teams are named the Wolfpack. There, a sculpture of wolves honors the campus icon. The artist hoped it would inspire students to achieve their goals.

The gray wolf is a popular image in artwork and photography.

INTO THE FUTURE

When gray wolves disappeared, conservationists realized that they were important to their **habitat**. Without wolves, elk herds in Yellowstone National Park grew very large. The elk ate too many aspen trees. Without aspen groves, songbirds lost nesting sites. Shade-loving plants lost growing sites. And, beavers lost a supply for building dams.

Wolves in Yellowstone share their habitat with buffaloes.

In 1995, a group of gray wolves was set free in the park. Rangers soon noticed changes. The wolves limited coyote and elk populations. Aspen groves thrived, and plants grew beneath the trees. Songbirds returned to nest and beavers built new dams. The ecosystem gained a new balance.

Today, the **IUCN** lists gray wolves as "least concern." In Minnesota, Wisconsin, and Michigan, they were taken off the **Endangered** Species List in January 2012. Minnesota allowed limited hunting of wolves beginning in the fall of that year. Hunters could take up to 400 wolves total during the season.

Scientists keep learning more about gray wolves. And, more groups are working to protect them. Ely, Minnesota, is home to the International Wolf Center. The Wolf Conservation Center is in South Salem, New York. Both organizations work to educate people about wolves.

Gray wolves have been saved from extinction. Conservationists believe living without wolves is worse than the challenges of living with them. Gray wolves are a symbol of nature's ability to renew. These icons help people learn to respect the wilderness.

GLOSSARY

breed - to produce offspring by reproduction.

Canidae (KAN-uh-dee) - the scientific Latin name for the dog family. Members of this family are called canids. They include wolves, jackals, foxes, coyotes, and domestic dogs.

continental - relating to the part of the United States made up of the lower 48 states.

cunning - getting what is wanted in a clever and sometimes deceptive way.

endangered - in danger of becoming extinct.

game - wild animals hunted for food or sport.

habitat - a place where a living thing is naturally found.

immigrant - a person who enters another country to live.

IUCN - the International Union for Conservation of Nature. The IUCN is a global environmental organization focused on conservation.

litter - all of the pups born at one time to a mother wolf.

pregnant - having one or more babies growing within the body.

regurgitate (ree-GUHR-juh-tayt) - to throw back out again, especially partly broken down food.

scavenge - to search through waste for something that can be used.

subordinate - placed lower in rank, class, or position.

WEB SITES

To learn more about gray wolves, visit ABDO Publishing Company online. Web sites about gray wolves are featured on our Book Links page. These links are routinely monitored and updated to provide the most current information available. **www.abdopublishing.com**

INDEX